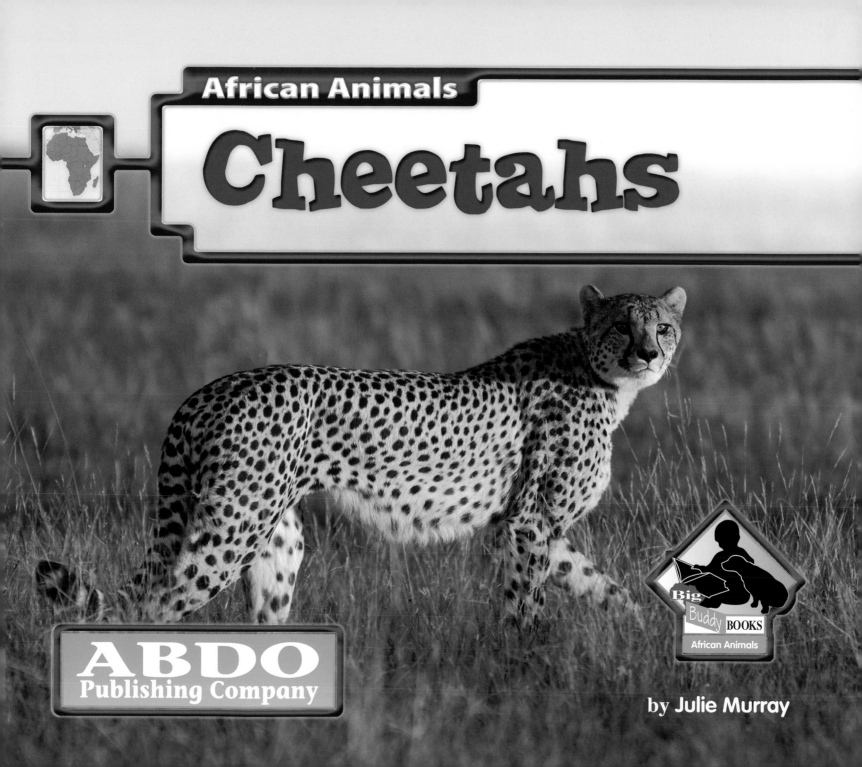

African Animals

Cheetahs

ABDO
Publishing Company

Big Buddy BOOKS
African Animals

by Julie Murray

VISIT US AT
www.abdopublishing.com

Published by ABDO Publishing Company, PO Box 398166, Minneapolis, MN 55439.

Printed in the United States of America, North Mankato, Minnesota.
102011
012012

♻ PRINTED ON RECYCLED PAPER

Coordinating Series Editor: Rochelle Baltzer
Editor: Marcia Zappa
Contributing Editors: Megan M. Gunderson, BreAnn Rumsch, Sarah Tieck
Graphic Design: Maria Hosley
Cover Photograph: *Shutterstock*: Jason Prince.
Interior Photographs/Illustrations: *Corbis* (p. 5); *iStockphoto*: ©iStockphoto.com/brytta (p. 4), ©iStockphoto.com/mddphoto (p. 7), ©iStockphoto.com/MissHibiscus (p. 9), ©iStockphoto.com/PTB-Images (p. 4); *Photolibrary*: Age fotostock (p. 8), Bios (p. 27), Bridge (p. 15), Eye Ubiquitous (p. 8), Imagebroker.net (p. 13), Oxford Scientific (OSF) (p. 21), Peter Arnold Images (pp. 19, 21, 23, 25); *Shutterstock*: Mark Beckwith (p. 17), Eric Isselée (p. 10), Alan Jeffery (p. 29), Ivan Kuzmin (p. 20), Christopher McRae (p. 11), palko72 (p. 9), p.schwarz (p. 15), Albie Venter (p. 29), Michael Wick (p. 11); *Stockbyte* (p. 9).

Library of Congress Cataloging-in-Publication Data

Murray, Julie, 1969-
 Cheetahs / Julie Murray.
   p. cm. -- (African animals)
 ISBN 978-1-61783-217-8
 1. Cheetah--Juvenile literature. I. Title.
 QL737.C23M878 2012
 599.75'9--dc23
                      2011030811

Contents

Long ago, nearly all land on Earth was one big mass. About 200 million years ago, the land began to break into **continents**. One of these is called Africa.

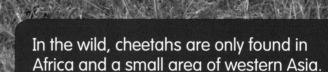

In the wild, cheetahs are only found in Africa and a small area of western Asia.

Africa is the second-largest **continent**. It is known for hot weather, wild land, and interesting animals. One of these animals is the cheetah. Cheetahs are known for their spotted coats and great speed.

Cheetah Territory

Most cheetahs are found in central, eastern, and southern Africa. They live in grasslands and open woodlands.

SAHARA DESERT

Nile River

▨ Cheetah Territory

Uncovered!
Long ago, cheetahs lived throughout much of Africa and Asia. Today, their territory is much smaller.

Cheetahs live in areas with tall grass so they can hide while hunting.

Jambo! Welcome to Africa!

If you took a trip to where cheetahs live, you might find...

...national parks.

Many African countries have set aside land for national parks. These areas help keep uncommon plants and animals safe. Many cheetahs live in national parks.

...farming.

About two-thirds of Africans make a living as farmers. Important crops include corn, wheat, and rice. Bananas, pineapples, olives, coffee, cocoa beans, and many other crops are also grown.

...grass-eating animals.

About one-third of Africa is covered in grasslands. So, grass-eating animals are common. These include antelope, wildebeests, and zebras. Some of these animals make good prey for cheetahs.

...many languages.

More than 1,000 languages are spoken across Africa! Swahili (swah-HEE-lee) is common in central Africa where cheetahs live. In Swahili, *jambo* is a greeting for visitors. *Masalala* means "goodness!" or "wow!" And *duma* means "cheetah."

Take a Closer Look

Cheetahs are members of the cat family. They have small heads and long, lean bodies and legs.

Yellow or tan fur with black spots covers most of a cheetah's body. White or light yellow fur covers its throat and belly. There are black rings at the end of a cheetah's tail.

A cheetah's spots are round or oval. They measure about one inch (2.5 cm) across.

Cheetahs (*below*) look a lot like leopards (*above*). But, cheetahs are smaller and have different spots. And, only cheetahs have black stripes running from their eyes to their mouths.

Adult cheetahs are two and a half to three feet (0.8 to 0.9 m) tall at their shoulders. They are six to seven feet (1.8 to 2.1 m) long with their tails stretched out. Adult cheetahs weigh 75 to 145 pounds (34 to 66 kg).

Uncovered!
Male cheetahs are a little larger than females.

A cheetah's tail is 25 to 35 inches (64 to 89 cm) long.

Built for Speed

Uncovered!
Cheetahs can sprint as fast as cars drive on a freeway!

Cheetahs are the fastest animals on land. They can sprint 70 miles (113 km) per hour for a short length.

Cheetahs reach top speeds quickly. They can go from standing still to running 60 miles (97 km) per hour in three seconds!

Cheetahs can only sprint for 200 to 300 yards (180 to 270 m). Then, they must stop and rest.

Cheetahs have special body parts that help them run fast. Their paw pads and strong claws **grip** the ground. Their long tails help them balance. And their nose shape helps them breathe easily while **sprinting**.

Uncovered!
Most cats can pull in their claws when they aren't using them. Cheetahs can't do this. Their claws are always out!

When a cheetah runs, its back bends easily. This helps its legs reach far with each step.

Great Hunters

Cheetahs are **carnivores**. They eat hares, gazelles, impalas, and other small- or medium-sized **mammals**.

Unlike most large cats, cheetahs usually hunt during the day. Their favorite hunting times are morning or early evening. Cheetahs see well in daylight. And, their spotted coats help keep them hidden in tall grass.

Cheetahs use their good eyesight to spot prey. Sometimes, they climb hills, rocks, and termite mounds (*above*) to see farther.

When hunting, cheetahs creep as close as they can to their *prey*. Then, they **sprint** after it and try to knock it down. A chase lasts just 20 to 60 seconds. And, cheetahs only catch their prey about half of the time.

When a chase is successful, a cheetah may drag its catch to a hidden spot to eat. If more forceful predators see a cheetah's catch, they will try to steal it!

Cheetahs are shy compared to lions (*right*), leopards, and hyenas. Usually, cheetahs back down if one of these predators tries to steal their food.

Uncovered!
Unlike many carnivores, a cheetah only eats prey it catches itself. And, cheetahs only eat meat. They do not eat fur, skin, or other body parts.

Cheetahs can turn quickly, even when sprinting. They use their tails to help them change direction.

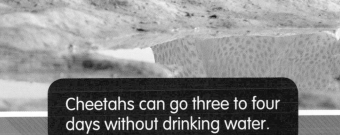

Cheetahs can go three to four days without drinking water.

Most cheetahs move freely around large home areas. But, some small groups of males stay in smaller territories. They mark these with their pee. And, they guard them against strangers.

Lonely Life

Cheetahs do not live in large groups. Adult females live alone or with their young. Adult males live alone or with a small group of brothers. Males and females only come together for short times to **mate**.

Baby Cheetahs

Cheetahs are **mammals**. Female cheetahs usually have two to five babies at a time.

Baby cheetahs are called cubs. At birth, cubs are less than one foot (0.3 m) long. And, they only weigh about ten ounces (284 g).

Cheetah cubs have dark fur.
And, their spots are not clear.
Their fur changes as they grow.

Cheetah cubs drink their mother's milk. For the first few weeks, they cannot see or walk. So, their mother moves them to a new hiding spot every few days.

After five to six weeks, cubs start to follow their mother around. They begin to eat meat from her prey. And, they learn to hunt by watching her. Cheetah cubs stay with their mother for one to two years.

Cheetah cubs have long, shaggy fur on their backs. This is called a mantle. Many scientists believe a cub's mantle helps hide it in tall grass.

Survivors

Life in Africa isn't easy for cheetahs. New buildings and farms take over their **habitats**. **Prey** is not as common as it once was. People kill cheetahs to keep them from hunting farm animals. And, they hunt them for their spotted coats.

Still, cheetahs **survive**. There are laws against killing them. And, many people are working to save their habitats. Cheetahs help make Africa an amazing place.

Uncovered!

Cheetahs are vulnerable. That means they are in danger of dying out. Scientists believe there are less than 10,000 adult cheetahs left in the wild.

Many cheetah cubs do not survive past their first few months. During this time, lions and hyenas hunt them. Other young cheetahs get sick and die.

In the wild, cheetahs live 10 to 12 years.

Masalala!
I'll bet you never knew...

...that cheetahs do not roar like lions and leopards. But they do purr, hiss, and growl. They also make a birdlike chirping noise to call family members. A cheetah's chirp is loud! It can be heard about one mile (1.6 km) away.

...that long ago, humans used cheetahs for hunting! This practice can be found in ancient African stories and drawings.

...that cheetah cubs practice their hunting skills on live **prey**! When cubs are about six months old, their mother catches small animals. She brings them alive to her cubs. Then her cubs practice chasing, catching, and killing them.

Important Words

carnivore an animal or a plant that eats meat.

continent one of Earth's seven main land areas.

grip to hold tightly.

habitat a place where a living thing is naturally found.

mammal a member of a group of living beings. Mammals make milk to feed their babies and usually have hair or fur on their skin.

mate to join as a couple in order to reproduce, or have babies.

prey an animal hunted or killed by a predator for food.

sprint to run at top speed for a short length.

survive to continue to live or exist.

Web Sites

To learn more about cheetahs, visit ABDO Publishing Company online. Web sites about cheetahs are featured on our Book Links page. These links are routinely monitored and updated to provide the most current information available.

www.abdopublishing.com

Index